The Adventures of Scuba Jack
Copyright 2021 by Beth Costanzo
All rights reserved

One of the most fascinating creatures in our oceans and seas today is the octopus. Most likely, you have seen a picture of an octopus in your favorite book on animals or even in your local aquarium. If you are lucky, you may have even seen an octopus as you were swimming in real life.

OCTOPUS

Whatever the case may be, the octopus is interesting for a whole host of reasons. Because of this, it is worth our time to explore what makes the octopus so fascinating. With these fun facts in mind, you can better appreciate the octopus's beauty and its role in our world. You can also use these facts to show your friends and family how smart you are.

So are you ready to join me in learning more about the octopus? Let's do it!

OCTOPUS

The Octopus: A Fascinating Sea Creature

The octopus is an absolutely fascinating sea creature for a number of reasons. But for most people, one of the most interesting things about octopuses is their appearance. It would be hard to disagree. The octopus is unlike any other animal that we see in our world. It is famous for its rounded body, bulging eyes, and, yes, its eight long arms. The octopus also has an extremely soft body that can rapidly adjust its shape. This ability is important because it lets the octopus squeeze through small gaps when avoiding predators, for example. For the most part, octopuses weigh between 6 and 22 pounds, have speeds of up to 25 miles per hour, and have lengths of about 1 to 3 feet.

Even though we just think of one type of octopus, there are actually around 300 different species of the animal. The largest known species of the octopus is the Giant Pacific Octopus, which can weigh around 33 pounds and have arms that reach up to 14 feet. The smallest species of octopus is called the Octopus Wolfi. This octopus is extremely small. It is only about one inch in length and weighs less than one gram. If you were swimming and one of these octopuses came close to you, it would be really hard to see.

OCTOPUS

Now let's talk about where you can see octopuses. Yes, if you visit your local aquarium or zoo, you will most likely see one or several. But if you are looking for octopuses in the wild, it is helpful to know where they will likely be. Generally speaking, octopuses live in every ocean, which is good news if you live next to the Atlantic or the Pacific Ocean. However, octopuses are more abundant in warm, tropical waters. For example, if you are going on vacation to Hawaii or some other warm climate, you are more likely to see octopuses in the wild. If you live near or are visiting a place with fresh water, however, you won't be able to see octopuses.

OCTOPUS

Octopuses like to eat many different kinds of fish. For example, they like to eat crab, shrimp, and lobsters. If an octopus is trying to eat a crab, for instance, it will inject that crab with a paralyzing saliva (which is a liquid from their body) and then eat the crab with its beak. Octopuses have to constantly be on the lookout for food, and when they find something worth eating, they strike.

OCTOPUS

Like all other sea creatures, the octopus isn't always safe in the water. There are animals in our oceans and seas that are trying to hunt octopuses for themselves. Most often, those animals are seals, whales, and large fish. Seabirds may also try to eat octopus. To protect itself from these predators, the octopus relies on several defenses. Like I said earlier, the octopus is slippery and can move quickly in the water. But beyond that, the octopus can shoot an inky fluid when it is being chased by a predator. The ink darkens the water around the octopus, which can confuse the aggressor. That confusion may buy enough time for the octopus to escape the predator's jaws. Finally, the octopus can evade predators through the use of camouflage. This basically means that the octopus can blend in with its surroundings, allowing it to hide from animals that may eat it. The octopus can change into colors like gray, brown, pink, blue, or green.

Compared to some other sea creatures, octopuses live pretty short lives. In fact, some species live as little as 6 months. On the other hand, the Giant Pacific Octopus can live for as long as 5 years. Octopuses live for such a short period of time because of the way that they are created. Male octopuses die shortly after they mate with females, while female octopuses die after their eggs hatch.

OCTOPUS

Finally, one of the coolest things about the octopus is that it is really smart. Some researchers discovered that octopuses can save both short-term and long-term memories. It can even be trained to tell the difference between certain shapes and patterns. Compared to other fish or marine life, the octopus is very smart—even though it learns nothing from its parents.

OCTOPUS

The facts above give you a really good idea of why the octopus is so special. It is one of the most fascinating sea creatures, whether you are simply looking at it or understanding how it escapes predators. To further impress your friends and family, here are some more fun facts about the octopus.

• The name octopus was first coined in the year 1818.
• Octopuses have excellent sight, allowing them to quickly spot food and avoid predators.
• Octopuses are considered to be a delicacy in many parts of the world (especially in Europe and Asia).
• The octopus has extremely large eyes. They are located at the top of its head.
• Octopuses can taste what they touch.
• The Giant Pacific Octopus can lay 10,000 to 70,000 eggs at one time.
• When they are not mating or hunting, most octopuses don't move.
• Octopuses generally try to avoid humans.

COLORING PAGE

WWW.ADVENTURESOFSCUBAJACK.COM

OCTOPUS PARTS

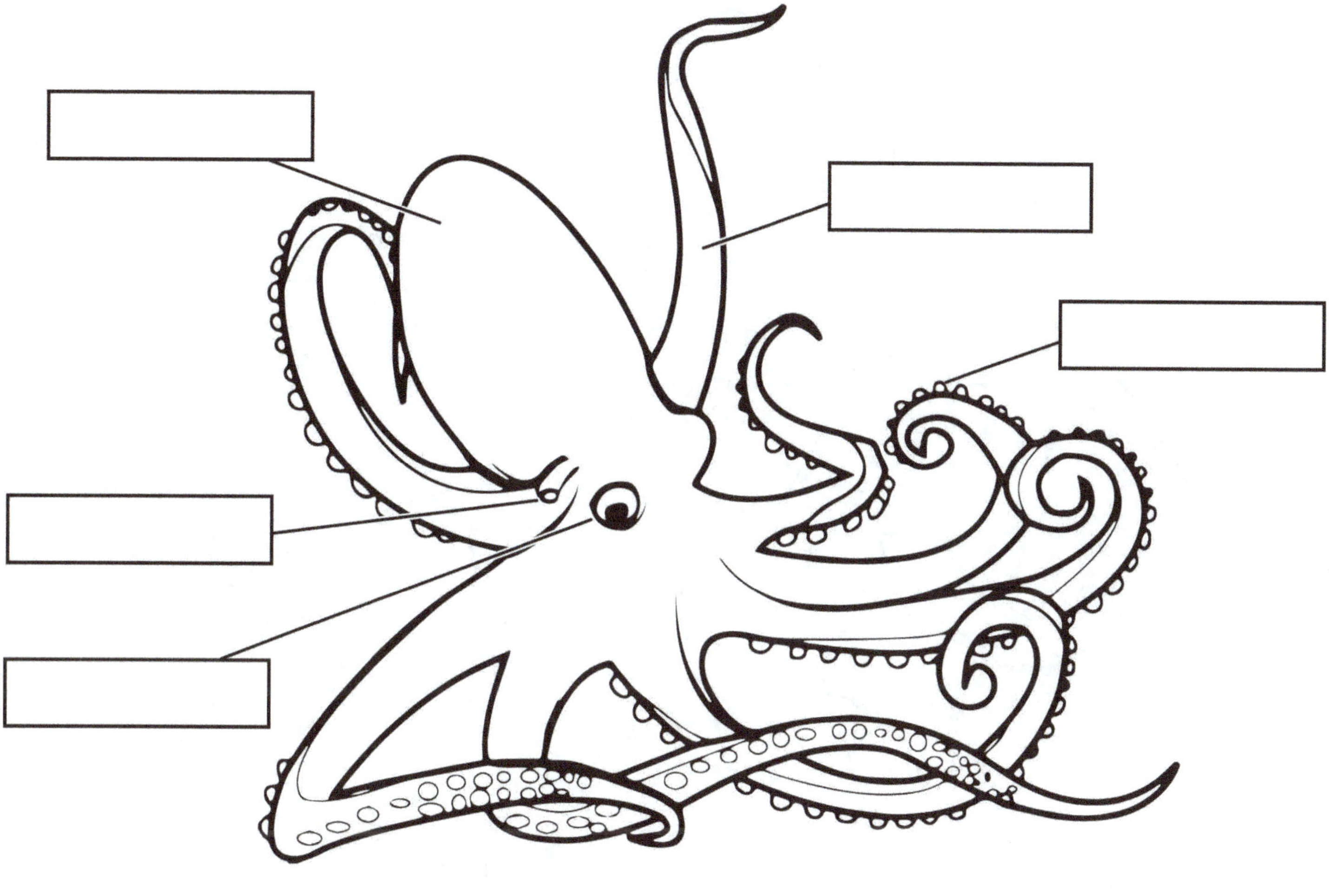

WORD BANK
mantle - eye - arm - siphon - suction cup

COLOR BY NUMBER

1 - blue   4 - orange   7 - pink
2 - purple   5 - purple   8 - brown
3 - green   6 - yellow   9 - red

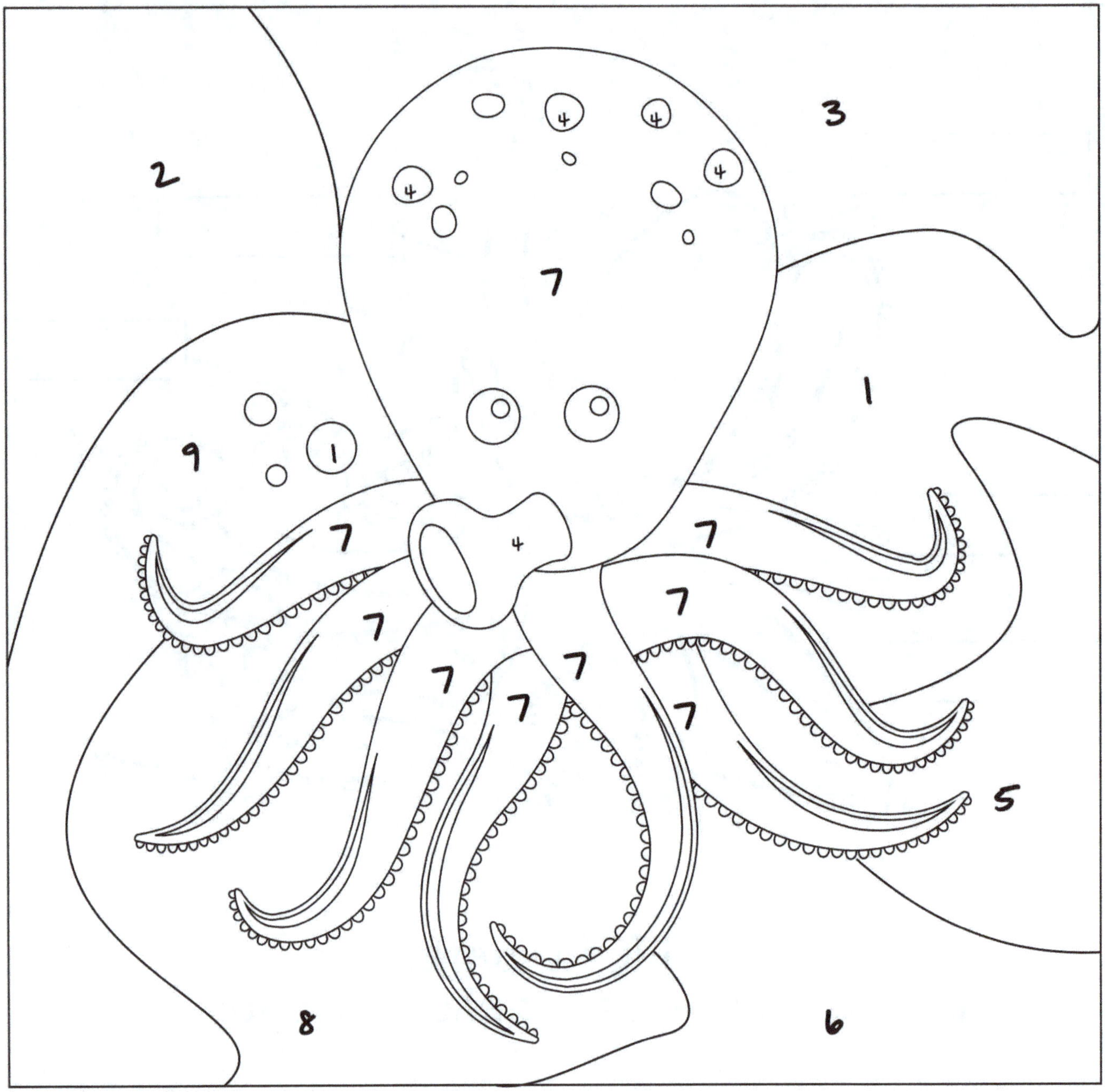

www.adventuresofscubajack.com

OCTOPUS DOT-TO-DOT

www.adventuresofscubajack.com

COLORING PAGE

WWW.ADVENTURESOFSCUBAJACK.COM

LETTER FIND

Make a circle around the letters of the word O C T O P U S

F A o P L M
m R d y X a f
k g Z r
h s T Q G
L g J
E i T e V
n h B
q b x
d U N O D m
H C V r
l j

WWW.ADVENTURESOFSCUBAJACK.COM

COLORING PAGE

WWW.ADVENTURESOFSCUBAJACK.COM

COUNTING PRACTICE

1   3   5   2

2   5   1   3

1   3   4   2

1   3   5   2

www.adventuresofscubajack.com

COLORING PAGE

WWW.ADVENTURESOFSCUBAJACK.COM

SHAPE RECOGNITION

Connect the drawings on the left side to the right shape on the right side.
Color the drawings on the left

WWW.ADVENTURESOFSCUBAJACK.COM

COLORING PAGE

www.adventuresofscubajack.com

OCTOPUS TRACING

octopus

octopus

octopus

octopus

WWW.ADVENTURESOFSCUBAJACK.COM

OCTOPUS MAZE

START HERE

exit

WWW.ADVENTURESOFSCUBAJACK.COM

Visit us at:
www.adventuresofscubajack.com

www.ingramcontent.com/pod-product-compliance
Lightning Source LLC
Chambersburg PA
CBHW060430010526
44118CB00017B/2430